SO-BZU-456

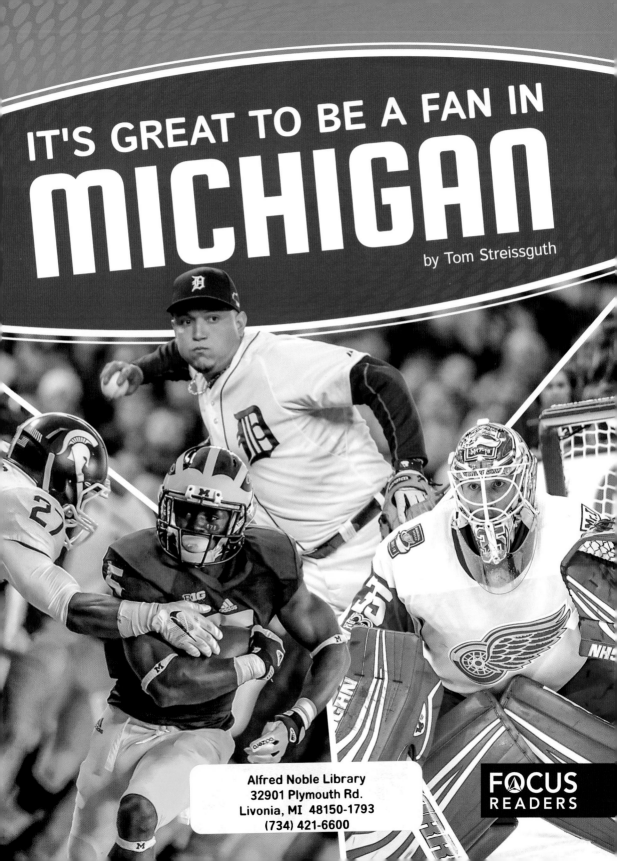

IT'S GREAT TO BE A FAN IN
MICHIGAN

by Tom Streissguth

FOCUS
READERS

FOCUS READERS

www.focusreaders.com

Focus Readers is distributed by North Star Editions:
sales@northstareditions.com | 888-417-0195

Produced for Focus Readers by Red Line Editorial.

Photographs ©: Paul Sancya/AP Images, cover (top), 1 (top); Lon Horwedel/Icon Sportswire/ AP Images, cover (left), 1 (left); Roy K. Miller/Icon Sportswire, cover (right), 1 (right); Jennifer Nickert/Shutterstock Images, 4–5; Library of Congress, 7, 11; Dieon Roger/Shutterstock Images, 9; Photo Works/Shutterstock Images, 12–13; Tigers Archives/AP Images, 15; Rick Osentoski/AP Images, 17; Michael Conroy/AP Images, 19; Red Line Editorial, 21, 43; AP Images, 23, 30–31; Aaron M. Sprecher/AP Images, 24–25; Carlos Osorio/AP Images, 27; Sue Ogrocki/AP Images, 33; Lorraine Swanson/Shutterstock Images, 35; Luca Santilli/ Shutterstock Images, 37; Steven King/Icon Sportswire/AP Images, 38–39; Gary Blakeley/ Shutterstock Images, 41; Tony Ding/AP Images, 45

ISBN
978-1-63517-931-6 (hardcover)
978-1-64185-033-9 (paperback)
978-1-64185-235-7 (ebook pdf)
978-1-64185-134-3 (hosted ebook)

Library of Congress Control Number: 2018931998

Printed in the United States of America
Mankato, MN
May, 2018

ABOUT THE AUTHOR

Tom Streissguth has written more than 100 works of nonfiction for young readers. He also founded the Archive of American Journalism, which publishes historic journalism collections for the use of students, teachers, and researchers. Streissguth has traveled widely in Europe, Asia, and South America, and currently lives in Woodbury, Minnesota.

TABLE OF CONTENTS

CHAPTER 1

GREAT LAKES AND WOLVERINES

Sports fans in Michigan have a lot to cheer for. The city of Detroit offers teams in every major professional league. Some of the country's most successful college sports programs can be found around the state, too. And no matter where they are, fans stand by their favorite teams through thick and thin. The state's unique sports culture reflects the region's history, geography, and economy.

The Tigers' Comerica Park offers sweeping views of the Detroit skyline.

Touching four of the five Great Lakes, Michigan's location and geography have helped it become one of the most populous states in the Midwest. The big waters divide the state into two large **peninsulas**, Upper and Lower. Forests and lakes cover much of the north, while southern Michigan is home to the state's largest cities and major industries.

American Indian tribes such as the Ottawa, Ojibwa, and Potawatomi have been living in Michigan for thousands of years. However, as white settlers arrived, they gradually pushed the tribes off their land. The first white people to arrive were **missionaries** and fur traders. Jacques Marquette, a French missionary, founded Sault Ste. Marie in 1668. In 1701, French explorer Antoine Cadillac built a fort and trading post on the future site of Detroit.

The Potawatomi tribe originally lived in Michigan but was forced west as white settlers came to the area.

The British captured Detroit from the French in 1760. They held the city until 1794, when a **treaty** gave the newly independent United States control. Two years later, the area became part of the Northwest Territory. And in 1805, Michigan became its own territory. Around this time, the United States and local tribes began signing treaties. In these agreements, the tribes gave up land for US settlements.

New settlers arrived to farm and trade. Settlement increased thanks to the Erie Canal in New York, which linked the Great Lakes to the East Coast. This helped Michigan settlers bring their goods to busy eastern markets.

In the early 1800s, there were still few roads leading to the territory. Maps had little detail. In 1835, one mapmaker's mistake nearly led to a war between settlers in Michigan and Ohio. The two sides argued over who should own the mouth of the Maumee River and the town of Toledo. According to one story, Ohioans nicknamed Michiganders "Wolverines" during this time. The

➤ THINK ABOUT IT

How do you think the Great Lakes shaped the settlement of Michigan in the state's early days?

Originally in Detroit, the University of Michigan moved to its current location in Ann Arbor in 1837.

wolverine is a feisty, bad-tempered animal that is always ready for a fight. The people of Michigan adopted the name with pride. The University of Michigan, which had opened in 1817, made the wolverine the **mascot** for its sports teams.

Michigan became a state in 1837. Its name comes from an Ojibwa word meaning “great water.” Throughout the early to mid 1800s, settlers cleared farmland in southern Michigan.

As the population grew, so did attendance at the state's universities. In 1865, the University of Michigan made baseball its first varsity sport. A varsity football team began playing in 1878.

The state's most important industry was born in 1899. In that year, Henry Ford built an automobile factory in Highland Park, a small city bordering Detroit. Ford's **assembly lines** allowed factory workers to make cars quickly. The company paid good wages for the time, and Ford priced his cars to make them affordable. This helped Detroit become the center of the US auto industry.

Eventually, competition from foreign carmakers hurt the auto industry. Many factories closed down. Michigan cities that depended on the auto industry lost jobs. Despite the hard times, Michigan's professional sports teams remained.

▲ Ford's affordable cars helped the auto industry take off, lifting Detroit's economy with it.

This helped them win the loyalty of fans throughout the state. In recent years, Michigan's economy has improved as new industries emerge.

Through good times and bad, sports have served as a rallying point for Michiganders. New stadiums have been built in Detroit. Meanwhile, Michiganders have teams to root for on all levels throughout the year.

CHAPTER 2

MOTOR CITY SPORTS

As a state, Michigan has gone through good times and hard times. But through it all, fans have remained loyal to their professional sports teams. The fans have been rewarded with some unforgettable wins, but they have also endured some terrible seasons.

All of Michigan's major teams are based in or near Detroit. And all four have a long history in their respective leagues.

Tigers first baseman Miguel Cabrera won Most Valuable Player Awards in 2012 and 2013.

The Tigers baseball team joined the American League (AL) in 1901. That was also the league's first year. The team has been around ever since. The Tigers' first home was Bennett Park, just west of downtown Detroit. The Tigers later built Navin Field at the same location. The ballpark opened in 1912. It could seat 25,000 people and had a tall flagpole in center field. The stadium expanded over the years and eventually became known as Tiger Stadium. In 1999, the team moved a few blocks into Comerica Park in downtown Detroit.

Through the different stadiums, the Tigers have won four World Series and featured some of the game's most legendary players. Ty Cobb was one of baseball's first stars. He played in the outfield for the Tigers for 22 years. Cobb broke just about every record in the books and achieved an incredible .366 career batting average. This

△ Tigers center fielder Ty Cobb (right) led the AL in batting average in 12 of 13 years from 1907 to 1919.

record still stands as the highest lifetime average in major league history. Other stars such as Hank Greenberg, Al Kaline, and Miguel Cabrera all wore the team's iconic caps, too.

Across the street from Comerica Park is Ford Field. The Lions football team moved into this indoor stadium in 2002. However, they have been playing in the National Football League (NFL) since 1930. The team moved to Detroit in 1934.

It had played its first four seasons in Portsmouth, Ohio, approximately 300 miles (480 km) to the south.

The Lions have had a mixed history. The team has won four NFL championships. However, the most recent one was in 1957. In the early 2000s, the team struggled through some tough seasons. In fact, the Lions became the first team to go 0–16 when they did so in 2008. Going into the 2018 season, the team had not won a playoff game since 1991.

Although the team hasn't always been great, the Lions have featured several great players. The Lions selected Barry Sanders in the 1989 draft. He went on to become one of the best running backs in league history. Sanders rushed for 15,269 yards during his 10-year career. With a strong and compact frame, Sanders could bowl

In the 2010s, Lions quarterback Matthew Stafford established himself as one of the NFL's best passers.

over defenders or pivot quickly to find running room down the field.

Calvin Johnson was a top wide receiver for the Lions from 2007 to 2015. For many of those years, he partnered with quarterback Matthew Stafford to form a dangerous duo. Stafford joined the team in 2009. Going into the 2018 season, he had passed for more than 34,000 career yards. That was by far the best in Lions' history.

The Pistons were founded in 1948 in Fort Wayne, Indiana. That was one year before the National Basketball Association (NBA) was formed. In 1957, the team moved to the Detroit area. The Pistons played in different arenas before moving to Little Caesars Arena in 2017. But no matter where they played, the Pistons have featured some great players.

One of the most memorable eras in Pistons history was in the late 1980s and early 1990s. Those teams were nicknamed the Bad Boys. Featuring tough players such as Rick Laimbeer, Dennis Rodman, and Isiah Thomas, the Pistons became one of the NBA's most dominant teams. They won back-to-back NBA titles in 1989 and 1990.

In the early 2000s, the Pistons became a power once again. That team didn't have any superstars.

▲ The Pistons won their third NBA championship by shocking the Los Angeles Lakers in 2004.

However, behind hard-working team players such as Chauncey Billups, Richard Hamilton, and Ben Wallace, the Pistons won another NBA title in 2004.

Hockey has a long history in Detroit, too. The Detroit Cougars joined the National Hockey League (NHL) in 1926. Four years later they became the Falcons. And in 1932, Chicago businessman James Norris bought the team.

Norris renamed the team the Red Wings. He also designed the famous winged red wheel. This logo has appeared on Wings jerseys since the 1930s.

Since then, few teams have matched the Red Wings' success. As of 2017, the team had won the Stanley Cup 11 times. The Wings were particularly dominant during the late 1990s. Featuring stars such as Nicklas Lidstrom and Steve Yzerman, the Red Wings won Stanley Cups in 1997, 1998, and 2002. The team also had an amazing streak of 25 consecutive years in which it made the playoffs, from 1991 to 2016.

Many great players have suited up for the Red Wings. Gordie Howe played 25 seasons in Detroit, starting in 1946–47. "Mr. Hockey" is remembered as one of the best players of all time. More recently, stars such as Pavel Datsyuk have upheld the team's tradition of greatness.

All four of Michigan's major league teams are based in Detroit. But before playing in Detroit, many athletes go through Grand Rapids. That's because the Pistons, Red Wings, and Tigers all have **farm teams** there. Minor league baseball teams in Lansing and Midland are also farm teams for other organizations.

DETROIT: A MAJOR LEAGUE CITY

75

Little Caesars Arena ○

Comerica Park ○

○ Ford Field

96

75

375

N
W ⊕ E
S

75

Detroit River

Downtown Detroit
○ Stadium locations
— Highways

JOE LOUIS

Joe Louis was born into a poor farming family in Alabama. The family soon came north to Michigan, where Joe's stepfather worked in a Ford auto factory. Joe's mother made her son try violin lessons to keep him out of trouble. But Joe didn't care much for music. Instead, he began training secretly at a local boxing gym.

Joe's boxing ability was hard to keep a secret. He worked hard for years in the ring. He developed the skill, strength, and stamina to match up with the city's best boxers. In 1934, Louis won the Detroit Golden Gloves light-heavyweight championship. Four years later, he won a first-round knockout over the German star Max Schmeling. Crowned heavyweight champion, the man nicknamed the "Brown Bomber" defended his title 25 times before retiring in 1949.

Joe Louis donated most of his prize money from boxing to different charitable causes.

Millions of fans followed Joe's fights over the radio. His string of victories inspired parades and celebrations, especially in his hometown of Detroit. In honor of Louis, the Red Wings named an arena after him. The team played in Joe Louis Arena from 1979 to 2017.

CHAPTER 3

THE COLLEGE GAME

Michigan college sports began at the University of Michigan in Ann Arbor. The school's baseball team played its first games in 1865. Football, basketball, tennis, track and field, and many other sports followed. The Wolverines became best known for football. But Michigan has one of the biggest and most successful athletic departments in the country.

Michigan and Michigan State are the two biggest colleges in the state.

Michigan State University in East Lansing is the state's second-biggest college. The school took its current name during the 1920s. At the time, Michigan State ran a contest to find a new name for its sports teams. A newspaper editor picked Spartans from among the entries. In ancient Greece, the Spartans were famous warriors.

Michigan and Michigan State play in the Big Ten Conference. This has created a heated **rivalry** between the two schools. Since 1953, the winner of their annual football game receives the Paul Bunyan Trophy.

However, the state's most famous football trophy is the Little Brown Jug. The trophy dates back to 1903, when Michigan left a water jug at the University of Minnesota after a game. Michigan asked to have it back. Minnesota's coach said the Wolverines would have to win it back.

Michigan has dominated the rivalry with Minnesota for the Little Brown Jug.

Michigan did, and over the years the Wolverines have won it back more than 70 times.

The Wolverines football team has had success against most teams. They have won 11 national championships and have the best all-time winning percentage of any team. The Wolverines also play in the nation's biggest football stadium. Michigan Stadium is nicknamed the Big House because it holds more than 100,000 people.

While Michigan is known for football, Michigan State has a history of great men's basketball teams. Earvin "Magic" Johnson helped establish that tradition. The point guard from Lansing led the Spartans to their first national title in 1979. Under coach Tom Izzo, the Spartans won another title in 2000. Izzo became known for having strong teams each season.

Men's hockey is also important for Michigan's colleges. The Spartans have won three national titles. But no team has won more than the Wolverines, who have nine national titles. The state also has six other **Division I** men's hockey

> THINK ABOUT IT

What are some reasons a person might decide to become a fan of a college sports team?

programs. They spread from Northern Michigan University in the Upper Peninsula to Western Michigan University in Kalamazoo.

College sports were limited mostly to men until the 1970s. Since then, Michigan schools have also had success in women's sports. The Wolverines have won national titles in field hockey and softball. The Spartans won a cross-country national title.

TALE OF THE TAPE ◄

Michigan Football	Michigan State Men's Basketball
First Season: **1881**	First Season: **1898–99**
All-Time Winning Percentage: **.728**	All-Time Winning Percentage: **.608**
Bowl Games: **45**	NCAA Tournaments: **32**
National Titles: **11**	National Titles: **2**

Accurate as of April 2018

CHAPTER 4

MICHIGAN ATHLETES

Michigan's sports tradition goes much deeper than college and pro teams. The state is also known for its youth and high school sports. Kids compete in a wide variety of sports, including golf, gymnastics, soccer, and swimming. And some have gone on to great success at higher levels.

Earvin Johnson attended Everett High School in Lansing, where he developed into a star.

Earvin "Magic" Johnson was a basketball star at his hometown Michigan State.

During his sophomore year, a sportswriter nicknamed the player "Magic." The name stuck. Magic Johnson went on to win a high school state championship at Everett and a college national championship at Michigan State. Later, he became an NBA star with the Los Angeles Lakers, winning five NBA titles and an Olympic gold medal.

Youth basketball is popular all over the state, but especially in Detroit. Future NBA stars Chris Webber and Shane Battier both played their high school ball at Detroit Country Day School.

Sisters Jennie and Meghan Ritter grew up in Dexter, which is just outside Ann Arbor. Both starred on the softball team at Dexter High School. And both went on to play for the University of Michigan. While there, Jennie Ritter became one of the best pitchers in the sport. She set many school records at Michigan. In

▲ Jennie Ritter pitches for Michigan in the 2005 Women's College World Series.

2005, Ritter led the Wolverines to victory at the Women's College World Series.

Many other great athletes grew up in Michigan. Tennis players Aaron Krickstein of Ann Arbor and Todd Martin of East Lansing both became top-10 players in the world. Golfer Meg Mallon went to high school near Detroit. She was later **enshrined** in the World Golf Hall of Fame.

One of Michigan's most famous athletes was Jerome Bettis. He played football for Mackenzie High School in Detroit before becoming a Hall of Famer as an NFL running back.

For all of Michigan's success in youth sports, the state is best known for its youth hockey. Boys and girls play the sport all across the state. However, the most successful programs are usually in the Detroit area. Many of these organizations carry the names of local companies that sponsor the teams. Michigan's top-level, or AAA, teams often compete for national championships. Several hockey players have gone from the state's AAA teams to college teams or the NHL.

Great young hockey players have another option in Michigan. In 1996, the US National Team Development Program (USNTDP) was

▲ Michigan had more than 50,000 youth hockey players in the 2016–17 season, second only to Minnesota.

founded in Ann Arbor. The best 17- and 18-year-old boys from around the country join this team. They train together and often play against older teams. The program, which is now in nearby Plymouth, is intended to develop top US players for the NHL and the Olympics. Among those who once played for the USNTDP are NHL stars Patrick Kane and Auston Matthews.

DYLAN LARKIN

Dylan Larkin has put together a uniquely Michigan hockey career. Growing up just north of Detroit, Larkin starred for the Belle Tire youth program. That led to an invitation to the USNTDP in Ann Arbor. After two standout seasons playing alongside some of the best boys his age, Larkin was ready for the next step.

The Detroit Red Wings selected Larkin in the first round of the 2014 NHL Entry Draft. Before joining his hometown team, though, Larkin suited up for his hometown college.

Larkin proved to be one of the nation's top scorers as a freshman at Michigan. So after just one season as a Wolverine, he jumped to the pro level. After spending some time with the Red Wings' minor league team in Grand Rapids, Larkin made his NHL debut on October 9, 2015.

▲ Dylan Larkin played for Team USA at the 2017 World Championships.

Just 19 years old, Larkin scored a goal and an assist that night. And it was only the beginning. During the 2015–16 season, Larkin scored more goals than any other Red Wing and made the NHL All-Star Team. He even won the speed contest at the All-Star skills competition and finished the year as the Red Wings **Rookie** of the Year.

CHAPTER 5

SPORTS, MICHIGAN STYLE

Michigan's rivalry with Ohio began long before football was invented. In 1835, the two states argued over borders during a dispute known as the Toledo War. In some ways, they never got over it. The rivalry spread to college sports when the University of Michigan and Ohio State University played their first football game in 1897. Michigan won that contest by a score of 36–0.

Michigan running back Chris Evans outruns an Ohio State defender during their 2017 game.

Michigan and Ohio State both became very successful. Today, they are two of the biggest college football programs in the country. So, when they meet each year, millions of fans tune in. The rivalry is so fierce that many people refer to it simply as The Game. Through the 2017 meeting, the Wolverines had 58 wins, 49 losses, and 6 ties.

Geography has played a major role in the rivalry's growth. Ohio borders Michigan to the south. For fans, it's only a three-hour drive from Ann Arbor to Ohio State's campus in Columbus. Several major roads connect the two states, including Interstate 75. Because of

> ## ➤ THINK ABOUT IT

How do you think the auto industry has affected Michigan's rivalry with Ohio State?

Detroit is a major economic and cultural center in the Midwest.

these connections, Michigan and Ohio have also developed close economic ties.

The United States' three largest automakers are based in the Detroit area. Workers at giant factories build the cars. And workers at other factories create the supplies to build the cars. Many of these factories are in Michigan. But nearby Ohio cities such as Akron, Cleveland, and Toledo help the automakers produce cars, too.

Detroit is Michigan's biggest city. It sits at an important location on the eastern side of the state, between the upper and lower Great Lakes. Because of this location, any boat traveling to or from Lake Huron, Lake Michigan, or Lake Superior must pass through the Detroit River. The city also has a major airport that connects to cities around the world.

Most of Michigan's population lives in the Lower Peninsula, which is shaped like a mitten. The Upper Peninsula (UP) lies to the north. A strait between Lake Huron and Lake Michigan separates the two peninsulas. However, cars and trucks can go from one peninsula to the other thanks to the Mackinac Bridge. The bridge, which is part of Interstate 75, spans nearly 5 miles (8.0 km). The I-75 freeway ends at Sault Ste. Marie, at the UP's northeastern border.

Although there are no major pro sports teams in the UP, sports are still important there. Winters are long and cold in the UP, and the "Yoopers" who live there favor winter sports.

MICHIGAN MAP

Although many Michigan fans cheer for the teams in and around Detroit, other cities with colleges and minor league teams are often closer.

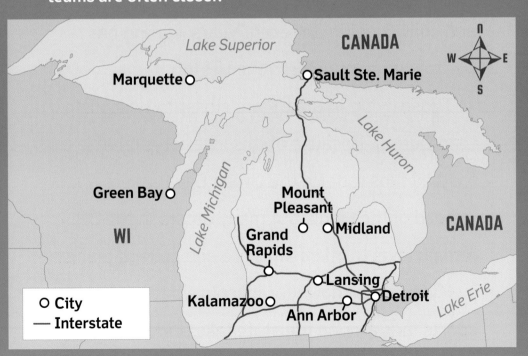

One of the biggest events each year in the UP is the I-500 Snowmobile Race. It takes place each February in Sault Ste. Marie. Riders speed their machines around an icy oval track. Some reach speeds of more than 100 miles per hour (161 km/h) on the straightaways.

The UP is also home to cross-country ski trails, skiing and snowboarding hills, as well as opportunities for activities such as snow tubing and snowshoeing. In recent years, curling has become more popular in the UP, too.

Those living in the UP are closer to Wisconsin than Detroit. Because of this location, some football fans root for the Green Bay Packers instead of the Lions. But many others in the UP remain loyal to Michigan's pro and college teams.

Michigan is known for its cold winters, and sports fans around the state take pride in the cold

Fans braved the cold to watch Michigan and Michigan State play an outdoor hockey game in 2010 in Ann Arbor.

weather. Football season starts in the late summer and ends during the coldest part of winter. That doesn't matter to the fans who **tailgate**. Whether they are cheering on the Lions or a college team, they gather in the parking lot before each game for a cookout. It is one of the many traditions that make it so fun to be a Michigan sports fan.

FOCUS ON
MICHIGAN

Write your answers on a separate piece of paper.

1. Write a sentence summarizing Michigan's youth hockey program, as described in Chapter 4.

2. Do you think a wolverine or a Spartan is a better symbol for a college sports team? Why?

3. Which professional team in Detroit was founded first?
   - A. the Lions
   - B. the Tigers
   - C. the Red Wings

4. Why might sports fans in the UP root for the Green Bay Packers?
   - A. Green Bay is the closest city that has an NFL team.
   - B. The UP used to be part of Wisconsin.
   - C. The Packers formerly played games in the UP.

Answer key on page 48.

GLOSSARY

assembly lines
Series of work stations organized in a line to put together the parts of a whole product.

Division I
The top level of college sports in the United States.

enshrined
Added to a hall of fame.

farm teams
Minor league teams that develop players for a major league team.

mascot
A figure used to represent a sports team.

missionaries
People who teach religious beliefs and attempt to convince others of those beliefs.

peninsulas
Bodies of land surrounded on three sides by water.

rivalry
An ongoing competition between two players or teams.

rookie
A professional athlete in his or her first year.

tailgate
To have a party before a game, often in the parking lot outside the stadium.

treaty
An official agreement between groups.

TO LEARN MORE

BOOKS

Gerstner, Joanne. *Detroit Tigers*. Minneapolis: Abdo Publishing, 2015.

Gitlin, Marty. *Michigan Football*. New York: Rosen Central, 2014.

Zweig, Eric. *Detroit Red Wings*. New York: Crabtree, 2018.

NOTE TO EDUCATORS

Visit **www.focusreaders.com** to find lesson plans, activities, links, and other resources related to this title.

INDEX

Answer Key: 1. Answers will vary; 2. Answers will vary; 3. B; 4. A